FIRST AMONG SEQUELS

by

Jim Badr

William Sessions Limited
York, England

Acknowledgements (Forward)
(*See also p.35 "Backward*)

My thanks to:

Judith, my wife, for inspiration, criticism and undaunted work
on the word processor;
Fran Badman, my daughter, for the colour illustrations;
My publishers for great patience;
All of you who bought "First Edition"; (We printed and I stapled
more than two thousand, a very successful fundraiser for
Somerton Summer Arts Festival, now in it's sixteenth year.)
All the people who spent thousands of years making the
Language so funny that poems write themselves;
The trees who made the paper.

I hope "First Among Sequels" maintains the standard of
galvanised irony and word play of "First Edition".

Any resemblance to poetry or verse and of characters to persons
living, dead or Geoffry Archer* are fortuitous and immensely
gratifying to the author.

Copyright © 2003 Jim Badman.
ISBN 1 85072 308 7

Printed in Times New Roman from Author's Disk by
Sessions of York, The Ebor Press, York, England

* Not Jeffrey Archer.

Contents

A tiger's an expensive pet
Especially when it eats the vet.
So if your tiger should be ill
Be careful, it puts up the bill.

FELIX DOMESTICAT

THE Puddy Tat, on paddy paws,
Knows nothing of our human laws.

SHE humours us, our funny ways.
But She is God, and we Her slaves!

SHE comes and goes, at her own choice
And orders with imperious voice.

WE think we know, we think she cares,
But it's not so – see how She stares.

SHE is still a wild thing.
Believe me not? Then hear Her sing!

IN the dark recess of Her mind
I dare not think what you may find.

MILLENIA of Teeth and Claws
Have no need of human laws.

McGonagal

McGonagal, McGonagal,
There's no one like McGonagal,
The more serious his subject
The more his verse is comical.
He writes of great disasters
With metre slightly erratic,
But he is sure you will find
His poetry charismatic.

McGonagal, McGonagal,
There's no one like McGonagal.
His use of words original
And never economical.
He chooses massive subjects
His poems are enormous
And quite unlike Robbie Burns,
He's never seen a dormouse.

McGonagal, McGonagal,
There's no one like McGonagal.
He writes of actual happenings,
A very chronic chronicle.
While other poets are in books
He gets inside our heads.
His rhymes are so outrageous
And his rhythm grimly treads.

McGonagal, McGonagal,
There's no one like McGonagal:
Thanks be to God.

Don't count your chickens till they come home to roost.

Breaking The Mould

I am a Penicillium
A little grey-green mould
And though my face is very young
My race is very old.

A billion generations
Before you men evolved,
By experiment and self-sacrifice
Our problem we had solved.

To save us from bacteria
Who feed in all your drains
To kill off all our enemies
We grew poison in our veins.

One man one day was careless
With a culture which he fed
And very soon it wore plus spores
And his bacteria were dead.

His master was a clever man
With dread we heard his voice,
"This mould will save untold men's lives:
This mould will have no choice!"

You have stolen our defences
Given nothing in return,
You think you own the rest of life
When will you ever learn?

He wanted to be a neurosurgeon but kept losing his nerve.

Our birthright took a billion years
You used it in a hundred.
Though Fleming wept a million tears
Don't you think you've blundered?

Oh man, Oh man, since you began
All you can do is destroy.
You waste the world, our miraculous world
As if it were merely your toy.

$$1/f = 1/u + 1/v$$

To photograph a Diplodocus
You need substantial depth of focus;
But for a Pterodacticable
A speed as high as practicable.

Rrrrrain

I don't regret her accent,
I don't regret the pain,
I don't regret Edith Piaff –
But I do regret the rain.

Even a clock-maker has to unwind sometimes.

3

Shot

I found a bit of lead today,
In my breakfast dish,
I chewed it and tasted it,
Not what one would wish.

I wondered where it came from:
Was it from a gun?
Where does all the lead shot go –
From killers having fun?

Spreading over countryside,
Ploughed into each field,
Eaten up by trusting birds,
What poisons will it yield?

We've banned the lead from petrol,
We're digging up lead pipes.
How long before we say "Enough"
To killing of all types?

Illiterate people should not make letter bombs.

Kilkenny Fire

When we were newly married
You showed me Ire-Land,
Where mysteries and wonders
Abound on every hand.

In the centre of Kilkenny
On the only bridge, we pause;
The fire alarm has sounded
And we wonder at the cause.

The Engine crosses east to west,
And after a short delay –
A Tender full of firemen
Rushes by the other way!

The Men were dressed so smartly,
For everyone to admire,
And the Engine highly polished,
But we never saw the fire.

Now we've been married nineteen years
With hardly a regret;
Except we never found out,
If the two things ever met.

Dancing reels is a good way to unwind.

5

My Beautiful Dutiful Daughter

I'm very proud of my daughter.
She learned all that I taught her,
Then very much more
So I can be sure
That she knows *what* to do, *when* she oughter.

Dancing Ledge

The sudden snarl was in my ear
Instantly I froze in fear
And slowly turned my head this way
My eyes on edge in twilight grey.

Walking, lonely, unprepared
An ancient trackway to the sea,
Expecting wild teeth sharp and bared
Waiting to leap out at me.

But when my eyes had pierced the gloom
Along the raised bank by my ear
Two badgers sniffed to find out who
Or whom it was had most to fear.

(Dancing Ledge is a geographical site of quarrying
on the south Dorset coast.)

Vikings were Celts with a ship on their shoulders.

6

Pan to Mime

I find it somewhat tragic
That religions should be magic,
Which keeps the greater truth
From many that are born.

The ancient Hellene Mysteries
Are thought in solemn histories
To be built round nothing greater
Than a little ear of corn.

Don't do your conscience violence
But sit in loving silence
To find the living truth:
The rose grows on the thorn.

Cre-Asian Myth

Black man, brown man, yellow man, white.
Which colour's wrong and which colour's right?
When God made mankind many years ago
What did he expect as he over-cooked his dough?

For God creation was a bit experimental
And though he loved his creatures he was not sentimental.
The under-cooked were white and the burnt ones black;
But he made some lovely brown ones once he'd got the knack.

So we see that good and bad are rarely black and white,
And science and theology are as often wrong as right.

Fringe Medicine is nothing new: It was invented by medieval barbers.

Morals for Mortals

Grandpa would stand on his head –
He broke his neck and so is dead.
Thus he has learned that now he's old
It's best to do as he is told.

Cal-Horrific

They say I'm anorexic –
I know I'm very fat!
We don't agree on many things,
Certainly not on that.

The vicar says I'm wicked,
To starve myself is sinning.
But a girl must be beautiful –
I'm more Thinned against than Thinning!

Ascetics go without: Mystics go within.

Camp Site

When you arrived you were pink,
But you departed tanned.
The grass is pale where your tent stood
Compared with where I stand.

We spent our time in walking
And swimming in the sea;
But Oh how sad this site is,
Now you have gone from me.

Bedroom Window

A single tear runs down the pane,
The weather's "none too warm" again
And I from you aloof remain.
We go our separate ways.

If through the glass we could but see
The likeness there of you to me
And learn to bend the stubborn knee,
We might be whole again.

He used to be a meteorologist but could not stand the pressures.

Early To Bed, Early To Rise

Trad,
Uncle Bob and Aunty Mabel
Fainted at the breakfast table.
Newly-weds should heed this warning,
"Do not do it in the morning".

Add
Uncle Bob and Aunty Mabel
Did it on the breakfast table.
Things ain't always as they're painted,
'Twas the serving maid that fainted.

And
Aunty Mabel and Uncle Bob
Broke the table on the job.
If they want to have some more
They must do it on the floor.

Royalties

The Noble Duke of York,
He had ten thousand men:
But if his wife has just the one –
The papers all know when.

Roundabouts work - there are no two ways about it.

More Wind Than Waves

You know what I mean
By "You Know", you know?
You know what I mean
By "You Know"!
I'll spell it out clearly
So you'll know what I mean:
Then you'll know what I know –
You know?

November The Third

I fired a rocket in the air,
It fell to earth I knew not where.
'Twas only later that I found
My neighbour's house burned to the ground.

"Who is my neighbour?" Jesus asks,
Thus setting us tremendous tasks.
If we had lived the way he said,
There'd be less rockets - and less dead.

He used to crack jokes - with his teeth.

Pippa's Song

After the rain
Here come the snails.
Collect them in buckets
Collect them in pails;
But don't throw them over
Your neighbour's fence.
I find they return
Much hungrier thence.

Cer Taint Y

There is no-one so sincere as a bigot
His sepulchre as white inside as out.
The Cardinal Sin, for a man like him
Is to have the slightest little bit of doubt.

Crop Circles are made by cereal killers.

Coill na Stille

So many trees to please the eye,
A meadow where it's sweet to lie,
A country lane that's curving by,
And peace and contemplation.

The sunlight sparkling on the lake,
With time to give and time to take,
No rush to sleep nor need to wake,
Oh save us from temptation.

Often when by life I'm pressed,
Or by other's actions am distressed,
Indeed when I am plain depressed
I think of Coill na Stille.

Then though the world remains a mess,
And what to do is just a guess,
The troubles on me weigh much less,
When I think of Coill na Stille.

Hikers in boots believe in the transmigration of soles.

Ireland of the Welcomes

A petrol pump was needed,
Our tank was very low,
In Waterville we found one:
But one thing we did not know.

The pump was not "self-service",
Had only one grade fuel
And was worked by manual labour;
A museum piece, a jewel!

We asked the willing pump boy
If he knew the fuel's "octane",
He looked blank and puzzled,
So we hastened to explain.

When told of the "stars" rating,
With his hand on the handspike,
A slow smile spread across his face –
"How many Stars would you like?"

Late for Meeting Long Sutton, 1982

Friends
The Lord on whom we wait
Would have us make no fuss –
Except that we should not be late:
For then He waits on us.

Baptism can give you a bad name.

14

Go n-Éirí an Slí Leat

I tell myself "Statistics"!
I tell myself "God Saves"!
But I'm not so sure of either,
As you fly above the waves.

Separation joins us,
More firmly than before,
Strengthens our togetherness,
Increases love in store.

When you come home safely,
It's time for much thanksgiving,
To whom we give's uncertain,
But it must be to the living.

But now you are away again
I count nothing really sure;
I wait among my dreams until
You come home once more.

He who stops the buck carries the can.

15

Improvisation

My wife's face is beautiful
And like a poet's song,
When late for an appointment,
Made up as she goes along.

To Be Read Allowed

The King gave us a charter,
Many years ago,
To buy and sell and barter,
From stalls all in a ROW.

But that was many years ago,
It is quite different now.
The councillors have all said "no",
The stalls would cause a ROW.

Around the ancient document
They tied a pretty BOW,
And for their wise pronouncement
The council took a BOW.

Swearing is rarely original: There are usually precursors.

I.R. & U.V.

I have a loathing,
For clothing,
The less that I wear it,
The more I can bare it.

California 1995

Snowy Egrets,
Have no regrets,
They think it right
To be so white.

Averse To Verse?

I'm not ashamed of rhythm;
I'm not ashamed of rhyme;
I find them very helpful,
And use them all the time.

People of past ages
Remembered hours of verse
By means of rhyme and rhythm –
You could do much worse.

Acupuncture is holistic.

Burns Night

I do not wish to see
Myself as others see me.
I fear 'twould change my life so much
I simply wouldn't be me.

Dissolution or Disillusion

Clonmacnoise
Has lost its voice.
All its bells
Are somewhere else.

Clonmacnoise is an ancient group of ecclesiastical buildings
on the banks of the River Shannon with a very peaceful
atmosphere.

Are fibreglass skis glass slippers?

18

Flower Power U.S.A.

Whoever asked the question,
Which I think is rather odd,
"Oh did we come from monkeys
Or did we come from God?"

Now D.N.A. is complex
And the universe is big
And the only fruit of the fig tree
Is normally the fig.

So if any of you feel clever
And dogmatic about the flood,
Try rolling a daffodil flower
Back into it's bud.

Dogma British Style

The theology student asked "Which
Of this great pile of books shall I ditch?
My memory's poor,
The subject's a bore,
And Dog-Ma I find is a bitch."

Very religious people go on advanced retreats.

A Quaker Studies Comparative Religion

The Calvinist is predestinate,
And over Sinners gloats;
The C of E knows the Trinity,
But the Quaker knows his oats.

The Presbyters decide in Kirk,
By democratic votes,
While Cardinals rule the Catholics,
But the Quaker knows his oats.

The Mormon knows his scriptures
And from the Bible quotes;
And baptises his Ancestors!....
But the Quaker knows his oats.

The Baptists cross the Jordan
By wading or in boats,
He lost his head over a girl you know,
But the Quaker knows his oats.

The Methodists are sober men
And abstinence promote;
Saint Benedict now burns in Hell!
But the Quaker knows his oats.

There has been a staggering increase in drunkenness.

The Pentecostals speak with tongues,
And larynxes and throats,
The breath of God is in their lungs,
But the Quaker knows his oats.

The Brethren will never bet
On dogs or pools or totes,
Avarice is a mortal sin,
But the Quaker knows his oats.

Remember our youngest brother,
And his multicoloured coat?
We knew how to work a colour bar!
But the Quaker knows his oats.

The Patriarch has lots of sons,
And on every one he dotes,
He knows they will a nation make,
But the Quaker knows his oats.

The Shepherds saw an Angel,
While keeping sheep from goats,
And knew it meant a Newborn King,
But the Quaker knows his oats.

The Preacher extols the Widow,
With her mite (or was it groat),
He knows She will go to Heaven,
But the Quaker knows his oats.

The Somerset Land Drainage Authority lowers the Tone.

The Children in the Sunday class,
Learn Scripture still by rote,
To confirmation next they pass,
But the Quaker knows his oats.

The Student learns Theology,
By taking copious notes –
And Hippies "get Religion",
But the Quaker knows his oats.

The Soul of the Saint leaves this vale of tears,
And up to Heaven floats,
In his flesh will he see God.
But the Quaker knows his oats.

Bishops live in Palaces,
Surrounded by their moats,
And know their place - in the Hierarchy
But the Quaker knows his oats.

The Maharishi in his jet,
With wise words and anecdotes,
Knows how Crime may be reduced,
But the Quaker knows his oats.

The Missionary travels for his God,
And lives in lands remote,
Thus all the world knows Jesus Christ,
But the Quaker knows his oats.

Innumerate people just don't count.

Saint Francis, he loved animals,
Yes even rats and stoats,
Birds and Beasts and the Poor loved him,
But the Quaker knows his oats.

The Witch-doctor and the Alchemist
With their potions and antidotes,
Knew no Hippocratic oath,
But the Quaker knows his oats.

The Irish are religious,
(Apart from "beams" and "motes").
This Ulster holds a million guns.
But the Quaker knows his oats.

Now George Fox dealt in horses,
With sleek and shiny coats,
To keep them in condition
He would have to know his oats.

All oats once were wild,
Made like that by God,
And grew like that in Eden
Before plough e'er turned the sod.

Mediaeval punishments will continue while stocks last.

Resignation

I want a belly dancer,
If it's not too much to ask:
For people making festivals,
I should think a simple task.

I want a belly dancer,
I've hoped for one each year;
If I wait much longer,
'Twill be too late, I fear.

I want a belly dancer,
Though after all these years
I'm afraid if I make too much fuss
It's bound to end in tears.

I want a belly dancer.
Please tell me why not?
I know that they don't wear much –
But our weather's been quite hot.

I want a belly dancer,
Not much to ask, God knows;
With cymbals on her fingers,
And bells upon her toes.

Now a dancer is a fantasy
For many oldish men,
But why not see her "in the flesh"?
If only now and then.

I've told you a thousand times – avoid clichés like the plague.

I've wanted a belly dancer
Almost all my life,
And I'm a very fortunate man
To have a tolerant wife.

I want a belly dancer,
They're really quite respectable;
And I'd only lust a little
As I found her points delectable.

I want a belly dancer –
Not a can-can high-kick prancer.
I don't much like fish-net mesh –
I much prefer naked flesh.

I want a belly dancer
With face and form exotic,
Because it is an art form
So beautifully erotic.

I want a belly dancer
With a lithe pulsating body,
Compared with which "Madonna"
Is really rather shoddy.

I want a belly dancer
With almond eyes like sloes,
And all her flesh a-trembling
From her navel to her nose.

The Cyclotron is a tour de force.

I want a belly dancer,
An Egyptian or a Greek,
When her thighs and my eyes
Would play rhythmic hide and seek.

I want a belly dancer,
But I don't know how I'd pay –
Except she'd be so welcome
'Twould be not work but play.

I want a belly dancer,
With a body almost nude.
Eat your heart out Sigmund Freud
(You spell that Sigmund Freud)!

I want a belly dancer
They cannot be ignored –
Have you seen their audience
Ever looking bored?

I want a belly dancer
To dance by candle light;
Her gold and silver coins
To sparkle through the night.

I want a belly dancer,
In control of every sinew.
This hypnotic vision
Surely now will win you.

Political Sweeteners are Candied-dates.

I want a belly dancer
As a cure for my arthritis.
The exercise is good for her –
And good for me the sight is.

I want a belly dancer
With face and form divine,
Together with the fantasy
That she is truly mine.

I want a belly dancer,
I find her so entrancing:
I'm hypnotised and mesmerised
When I see her dancing.

I want a belly dancer,
But it's very clear to see
That it's terribly unlikely
That the dancer would want me.

July 2002

I had a belly dancer.
She took me off to bed.
Her name was Klebsiella!
I was very nearly dead.

Due to the greenhouse effect the human race ended in a dead heat.

Simple Gifts for the Twenty First Century

'Tis the gift to be loving, 'tis the gift to be Gay,
'Tis the gift to accept one another anyway;
And when we are ourselves with no pretence,
Then we shall find that our lives make sense.

When Simple Truth we all gain,
There'll be no more excuses, no need to explain.
To love one another will be our delight,
Till by loving, our living will come round right.

Kellogged

You've heard of "Moral Fibre",
Well, that's how it all began,
When Seven Days Advent Kellogg
Invented Cornflakes and All-Bran.

Ready to greet his Saviour,
Pure outside and in;
With a colon free of flatulence
And a soul quite free of sin.

"You can't serve God and Mammon"
Said the prophet - but it's odd,
They sell the stuff for profit!
Can Mammon thus serve God?

Is a think tank of sceptics a sceptic tank?

The Devil Goes To Meeting

The poorer Friends were sweeter,
But the richer Friends were fatter,
I therefore went to Meeting,
To carry off the latter.

The Clerk rose up to greet me
And welcomed me to meeting;
I looked around with pleasure
And thanked her for her greeting.

The Elders and the Betters
Along the front were seated,
I sent my spirit out for them –
And from it they retreated.

But one there was, a wild man,
Who dressed in leather breeches,
He sensed my spirit's presence
And rallied them with speeches.

He spoke for several hours
And ere he had concluded,
I left the Meeting quietly.
I wonder Friend, what you did?

(With apologies to Thomas Love Peacock.)

History is bunk: there's no future in it.

Two Minutes

Who chose two minutes?
Was it a politician
For whom silence means disapproval?

Who chose two minutes?
Some who would not fight
Are whole for a silent hour every week.

Who chose two minutes?
It takes about that long to die
Of bleeding, or asphyxiation,
Not of instant destruction,
Nor of radiation.

Who chose two minutes?
As a child it seemed long
As we gathered in the school hall
To honour those who died
In the "War to end War".

Who chose two minutes?
It seems long now
Only by comparison
With the time taken to press a button.

Shall we be silent four minutes,
To remember us?

Do we have any rights left?

Love Song

My garden's full of old man's beard
Where once the lad's love grew
And though I'm grey, my love has grown
Since the day you became my own:
Old age is not what once I feared
If I live and love with you.

My garden's full of changing light
With daylong moving shade.
I watch you as you pick sweet pea
So much I care you ravish me:
Your smile it fills me with delight
And for it I was made.

To This I Am Moved

Here and Now is The Kingdom.
Here we are in The Garden.
If I am cast out it is by my own will.
Love is Infinite and fills all Creation.
Christ came not to teach of death but to Live Life.
We can Live this same Life.
Here and Now is The Kingdom.

The Holy Spirit does not come Duty Free.

Ordinates

Newton was no gardener
Because he did not know
"What goes down, comes up again".
Applies to things that grow!

Evil Lution

A dozen dozing Dodos
Sleeping in the sun.
A sailor came and caught them all.
Then there were none.

Enginuity

Isambard Kingdom Brunel
Went to inspect his new Tunnel.
But he got such a fright –
They had built it upright:
So he said "I've invented the Funnel"!

Policemen in helicopters get ideas above their station.

The **S** word in the **S** tone
The Elements of Magic

The magician slept in the sunshine.
He dreamed that the rocks on which he rested,
and which his face grew to resemble,
could be changed into precious metal.

He devised a spell:
Take the rocks, and break them, and grind them
to restore them to the Earth their Mother.
Take fire and mix well with the earth.
Use air to feed the mixture until it is
as hot as the Sun the Father of Fire.
When the spirit of the rock is released
catch it in a shape in the earth again.

With the strength of your arm
use fire and water to temper the spirit of
the earth.
Sharpen it on a rock; sparkling rock,
which reflects the light of the fire.

The Sword has been released from the Stone!
The magician's stone;
The transmuting stone,
The philosophers stone,
which gives the power of death.

He woke and dreamed of the elixir of life.

**EARLY TO BED
EARLY TO RISE**

NCLE BOB and aunty Mabel
fainted at the breakfast table.
LET this be a dreadful warning
not to do it in the morning.

NCLE BOB and aunty Mabel
did it on the breakfast table.
THINGS aint always as they're painted
t'was the serving maid that fainted.

UNTY MABEL and Uncle Bob
broke the table on the job.
IF THEY want to have some more
they must do it on the floor.

Notes (Backward)

Verse one of "Uncle Bob and Aunty Mabel" was sent by my mother-in-law, Doreen Foley (née Edmundson), to try to shock me. So I added two more verses to try to shock her, but Quaker schools and art study in Paris had rendered her unshockable.

"Resignation" was my resignation speech from the committee of the Somerton Summer Arts Festival, where, each year, I suggested and they accepted, a belly dancer, but never booked one.

Last year, when they did, I was in hospital with blood poisoning. Violent vomiting is a sort of belly dancing and the cause was Klebsiella, fortunately cured by antibiotics (but not pencillin).

"A Quaker Studies Comparitive Religion", or how many rhymes for "oats" are there? I read at Yearly Meeting at Lancaster in 1978. Although the fourth line is unchanging it's meaning subtly changes.

And Sideways Add-Verse Reaction

With so much low grade poetry about it is needful to
protect oneself from overload. Some of the established
do this by denigrating "verse" which I take to be that
which rhymes and scans.
Very good prose can be chopped into irregular lines
and called poetry, but why? Mediocre stuff can be
chopped similarly.
For a teacher to say poetry need not rhyme and scan is
acceptable, to say it should not is vandalism.
It is desirable for a pundit to admit to admiring a work
of art, but not to tell others what to admire. Though
with some recent poetry, music and visual art being so
ugly and obtuse, the temptation to instruct and to take
instruction must be very great.
But, please, I will make up my own mind, thank you.
I know the wonderful sensation of creating and can
often feel this in the work of others.

See "Averse to Verse?" on page 17.